P9-CRZ-900

DATE DUE

An Early Career Book

careers in
CONSTRUCTION

Gloria Ramos

photographs by
Milton J. Blumenfeld

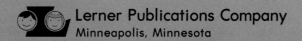
Lerner Publications Company
Minneapolis, Minnesota

LIBRARY OF CONGRESS CATALOGING IN PUBLICATION DATA

Ramos, Gloria.
Careers in construction.

(An Early Career Book)
SUMMARY: Briefly introduces such varied careers in construction as architect, interior designer, bricklayer, plumber,
elevator installer, cement finisher, and project manager.

1. Building as a profession—Juvenile literature. 2. Building
trades—Vocational guidance—Juvenile literature. [1. Building
trades—Vocational guidance] I. Blumenfeld, Milton J., illus.
II. Title.

TH159.R35 1975   690'.023   74-11903
ISBN 0-8225-0323-9

Copyright © 1975 by Lerner Publications Company

All rights reserved. International copyright secured. Manufactured in the United States of
America. Published simultaneously in Canada by J. M. Dent & Sons Ltd., Don Mills, Ontario.

International Standard Book Number: 0-8225-0323-9   Library of Congress Catalog Card Number: 74-11903

Second Printing 1976

690
R

Would you like to work in construction?

Construction, or building, is a very ancient trade. We can learn about peoples of the past by looking at what remains of the buildings they put up. One thing we learn is that the principles of construction have changed very little over the centuries. Most buildings still have internal frames and external shells. The rooms inside are built to serve certain functions.

Thus, the men and women who work in construction draw on experience that goes back thousands of years. Today, however, there are also many new tools and materials that construction workers can use. These things help make their jobs easier. Let's see how construction workers use old principles along with new tools and materials to put up a modern building.

114724

ARCHITECT

Architects design a building. First, they learn what the building is to be used for. It might be a bank, a concert hall, or a school. Then the architects make a model that shows how they think the building should look. If the people who are paying for the building like the model, they tell the architects to go ahead and draw plans for the building.

The plans show what the building will look like, inside and out. The floor plans show where every room will be on every floor. They show where windows and doors will go. With the help of engineers, the architects decide where to put electrical wiring, heating, and plumbing. The architects' plans will be used to guide the workers who build the building.

INTERIOR DESIGNER

The interior designer works with the architects to plan the inside of the building. He or she helps the architects decide how the rooms in the building will best serve the functions they are meant to serve.

Interior designers plan the carpeting, window covers, and furnishings of the rooms. They know how to make rooms pleasant places in which to work and live. For example, in a large office where many people will work, the interior designer will place desks and chairs so that the workers will have lots of space, light, and air. He or she will choose cheerful colors and comfortable furniture so that the workers will be happy in their surroundings.

ESTIMATOR

Estimators work for the building contractor. They help the contractor keep track of the costs of building materials. First, the estimators look carefully at the architects' plans. They find out how much wall space and floor space there will be. They look at all of the window and door measurements. Then, they figure how much the wood plaster, concrete, tiles, and other materials should cost.

Estimators talk to several different people who can supply these materials. These people give them bids, or cost estimates. When the estimators have looked at all of the bids, they choose the one that seems to be the fairest price.

Estimators must know mathematics very well in order to figure out costs accurately. They also must be good businesspeople so that they can get the best materials for the lowest cost.

PROJECT MANAGER

After the building has been planned, it must be put up. A building contractor owns a company that constructs buildings according to architects' plans. The project manager works for the building contractor. He or she oversees every step of the construction process, from beginning to end.

The building contractor's company builds the framework of the building. But there are also other jobs to be done. So project managers hire several different companies called sub-contractors. Each of these companies does a special job like putting in plumbing or wiring. The project manager sees to it that all of these jobs are done well and on time. He or she also makes sure that the labor and supplies for the building are paid for.

Project managers must know a great deal about all phases of construction. They often get their early training in engineering schools.

SITE SUPERINTENDENT

The site superintendent works at the actual building location. He or she makes sure that the workers are doing their jobs according to the architects' plans. Site superintendents know how to read the plans. They can tell if the walls, floors, and windows are being built the way they should be.

Meeting daily and weekly deadlines is also the responsibility of the site superintendent. He or she knows that costs will get too high if the building is not finished on schedule. Therefore, the site superintendent must plan what each group of workers will do every day and every week. Long experience in the construction industry helps the site superintendent to make realistic deadlines and to meet them.

CARPENTER

Throughout history, people have built almost all of their buildings around some kind of wood frame. Even people who lived in tents used some kind of wood to hold up the tent covers.

Today, carpenters, or woodworkers, are still building wood framework for buildings. But this framework is now often temporary. In heavy construction (the construction of the large concrete buildings we see in this book), carpenters build forms into which the concrete is poured. When the concrete has been poured and has hardened, the carpenters take away the wood frames. Carpenters also install, or put in, the doors, windows, and wood trim for large concrete buildings.

Many smaller buildings, such as houses, are still built entirely of wood. Carpenters build not only the framework for these buildings, but also the walls, roofs, and outer coverings.

BRICKLAYER

Bricklayers, or masons, build walls and chimneys. They build anything that is made of brick or cement blocks. Like all skilled construction workers, bricklayers must go through several years of training. This training is called an "apprenticeship." All craftspeople must serve an apprenticeship before they can be called "skilled."

Bricklayers work very carefully to make sure that they are laying their materials in a straight line. In the picture, you can see that the bricklayers have put up a string from one end of the wall they are working on to the other. This string helps them keep the blocks straight and even. The bricklayers use "mortar," a mixture of cement, lime, water, and sand. This holds the blocks together. Bricklayers must work quickly so that the mortar does not dry before they get the blocks in place.

LABORER

The laborers on a construction site help all of the skilled craftspeople do their jobs more quickly and easily. Laborers mix and carry mortar for the bricklayers. They unload and carry wood for the carpenters. They also keep the construction site clean. They carry away unused tools and materials so that the skilled craftspeople can begin each new project on a clean site.

A construction laborer must be a strong person, for he or she must lift and carry many things. As time passes, laborers learn a lot about constructing a building. Sometimes they may want to move up in rank and become skilled workers. When that time comes, the things they have learned about construction help them choose a specific craft like carpentry or bricklaying.

IRON WORKER

A poured concrete wall, by itself, may not be strong enough to support a building. Most concrete walls need to be strengthened from the inside. Iron workers, like the one in this picture, put steel rods inside concrete walls before the concrete is poured. After the concrete is dry, these rods will be hidden inside the walls of the building and will keep them strong.

Sometimes the frames of very tall buildings are made of huge steel beams. Perhaps you have seen them on an unfinished skyscraper. Iron workers put up these beams. This kind of work is very dangerous since the workers must walk the narrow beams hundreds of feet above the street.

When a building is almost finished, iron workers install all of the metal "finishing touches." They put in metal window frames, stairways, and handrails.

EQUIPMENT OPERATOR

For those who are fascinated by machinery, working with the giant machines on a construction site can be an interesting career. Equipment operators drive huge bulldozers and power shovels. With these machines they can dig large pits for building foundations. They can level parts of the land to make parking lots and walkways.

Equipment operators also drive trucks and cranes. The machine in this picture is called a tower crane. With it, the equipment operator can do many things. He or she can lift wood for the carpenters, iron and steel for the iron workers, and bricks for the bricklayers. Equipment operators and their machines help all of the workers in the construction industry.

CEMENT FINISHER

After the concrete has been poured into the frames the carpenters have built, it is left to harden, but not to dry completely. When the concrete becomes firm, the cement finishers begin their job. Cement finishers work with trowels, or special flat tools, to smooth the damp surface of the concrete. After the forms are removed, cement finishers fill in any cracks or holes in the concrete walls.

Concrete is not easy to work with. If the cement finishers begin their job too soon or too late, concrete floors may not be perfectly smooth and strong. Therefore, the cement finishers must know exactly what kind of "mix" they are working with. Then they can time their work properly. They make sure that the concrete supplier mixes the right kind of concrete for the job they are doing.

ELECTRICIAN

All electric heating, lighting, and air conditioning in a building is connected to many wires, which are hidden inside the building's walls. Electricians install all of the wiring needed to bring electricity to a new building.

Electricians put wiring for large buildings inside the poured concrete walls. This wiring is protected by a special metal "sleeve" called a conduit. When they install conduits inside walls, electricians make sure that part of the conduit sticks out of the wall. When the building is finished, the electric appliances will be hooked up to boxes that cover the conduits and the wiring.

Electrical wiring can be dangerous when it has not been put in properly. Thus, electricians must do their work carefully. They must follow strict safety rules.

PLUMBER

All of the water that we drink and wash with comes to us through pipes. Waste water flows out of our buildings through pipes, too. Pipes also carry the gas that we use for cooking and heating. Plumbers are skilled craftspeople who install all of the necessary piping in a building. They also install fixtures like drinking fountains, sinks, and toilets.

Like all skilled craftspeople, plumbers must know how to read architects' drawings. These drawings tell them where to put the pipes. Plumbers must also know how to cut pipes and how to connect them.

ELEVATOR INSTALLER

When architects plan a tall building, they always plan for elevators and elevator shafts. Elevator shafts are open passages that reach from the bottom floor to the top floor of a building. Elevator installers put the elevators in these shafts.

First, the elevator installers put guide rails in the shaft to hold the elevator car in place as it moves from floor to floor. Then they install the elevator motor at the top of the shaft and attach the elevator car to it.

Elevator installers test the cars in many ways to make sure they are safe. They even let them fall from the top all the way to the bottom of the shaft. Then they know whether the elevators will stand up under the impact of a fall. Elevator installers also make sure that the cars stop in just the right place on each floor of the building.

SAFETY SPECIALIST

Construction workers often walk on narrow platforms high above the ground. They use large tools and heavy machines. If safety rules are followed, a construction site can be a very safe place to work. If they are not, construction work becomes dangerous. The person responsible for safety on the construction site is the safety specialist.

The safety specialist teaches the workers about safe work habits. He or she makes sure the workers are wearing hard hats, safety glasses, and other protective equipment. The safety specialist also checks the job site for dangerous conditions.

Safety specialists are skilled in first aid, too. They know how to move an injured worker out of the way of danger until medical help arrives.

Construction careers described in this book

Architect

Interior Designer

Estimator

Project Manager

Site Superintendent

Carpenter

Bricklayer

Laborer

Iron Worker

Equipment Operator

Cement Finisher

Electrician

Plumber

Elevator Installer

Safety Specialist

A letter from a construction executive

knutson construction company

John O. Goodwyne
President

Dear Readers,

After reading this book, I hope you have a better understanding of how buildings are built and the types of jobs that are available in the construction industry.

The construction industry, which is the largest industry in our country, is made up of many contractors building many different kinds of projects, such as high-rise apartment and office buildings, dams, roads, power plants, warehouses, factories, and homes. There is great diversity in the industry and many job opportunities, especially for those people who like to build and who enjoy working outside.

Sincerely,

John O. Goodwyne
President

The publisher would like to thank the Knutson Construction Company, Minneapolis, Minnesota, for its cooperation in the publication of this book.

The photographs in this book realistically depict existing conditions in the service or industry discussed, including the number of women and minority groups currently employed.

We specialize in publishing quality books for young people. For a complete list please write

LERNER PUBLICATIONS COMPANY
241 First Avenue North, Minneapolis, Minnesota 55401